OPIOIDS AND OPIATES:
THE SILENT EPIDEMIC

Chronic Pain and Prescription Painkillers

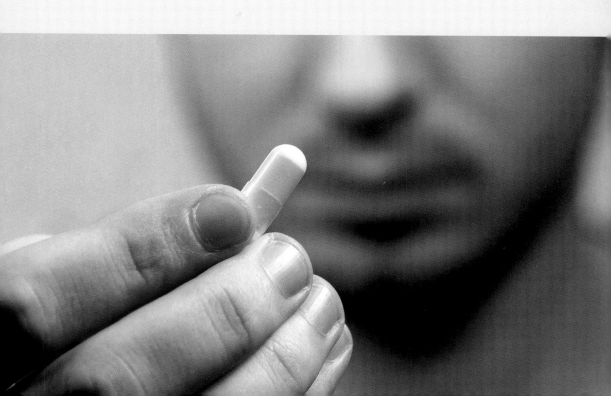

YOU ARE NOT ALONE

OPIOIDS AND OPIATES:
THE SILENT EPIDEMIC

Chronic Pain and Prescription Painkillers
The Dangers of Drug Abuse
The Heroin Crisis
Preventing and Treating Addiction
Who Is Using Opioids and Opiates?

OPIOIDS AND OPIATES:
THE SILENT EPIDEMIC

Chronic Pain and Prescription Painkillers

GRACE FERGUSON

MASON CREST
PHILADELPHIA

Mason Crest
450 Parkway Drive, Suite D
Broomall, PA 19008
www.masoncrest.com

Printed and bound in the United States of America.

CPSIA Compliance Information: Batch #OPO2017.
For further information, contact Mason Crest at 1-866-MCP-Book.

First printing
1 3 5 7 9 8 6 4 2

Library of Congress Cataloging-in-Publication Data

on file at the Library of Congress
ISBN: 978-1-4222-3823-3 (hc)
ISBN: 978-1-4222-7963-2 (ebook)

Opioids and Opiates: The Silent Epidemic series ISBN: 978-1-4222-3822-6

QR CODES AND LINKS TO THIRD-PARTY CONTENT

Table of Contents

KEY ICONS TO LOOK FOR:

 Words to understand: These words with their easy-to-understand definitions will increase the reader's understanding of the text while building vocabulary skills.

 Sidebars: This boxed material within the main text allows readers to build knowledge, gain insights, explore possibilities, and broaden their perspectives by weaving together additional information to provide realistic and holistic perspectives.

 Educational Videos: Readers can view videos by scanning our QR codes, providing them with additional educational content to supplement the text. Examples include news coverage, moments in history, speeches, iconic sports moments and much more!

 Text-dependent questions: These questions send the reader back to the text for more careful attention to the evidence presented there.

 Research projects: Readers are pointed toward areas of further inquiry connected to each chapter. Suggestions are provided for projects that encourage deeper research and analysis.

 Series glossary of key terms: This back-of-the book glossary contains terminology used throughout this series. Words found here increase the reader's ability to read and comprehend higher-level books and articles in this field.

 Words to Understand in This Chapter

crisis—a serious event that can turn into a disaster or become destructive if it is not handled appropriately or in time.

mortality rate—the death rate, or a measurement of the number of deaths—especially when related to a specific cause.

prevalent—something that happens often, or is widespread.

risk factors—in medical terms, anything that increases someone's chances of developing injury or a disease.

Introduction to Chronic Pain

When people experience physical pain, they may decide to seek medical care. The health care professional attending to them performs a physical examination and run some tests to determine where the issue lies. Once they understand why the patient is in pain, some form of treatment—such as medication or physical therapy—is prescribed. The patient begins to heal, and eventually they are able to return to their daily life. For many people, this type of experience will comprise the majority of their interactions with medical professionals. For other people, the situation might not be so simple. Some people never fully heal, or the cause of their pain is never uncovered. Many of these people end up living with chronic pain.

What is Chronic Pain?

Chronic pain is pain that lasts from at least three to six months consecutively, or is present for three to six months non-consecutively, in a twelve-month period. For example, someone who experiences pain from January to June may have chronic pain, which is more severe than just a small ache or pain. Sometimes, chronic pain can be traced to a certain injury that

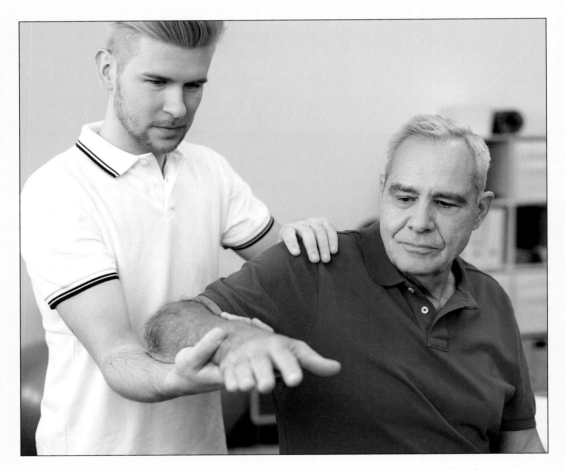

Acute pain is usually caused by physical injuries. This type of pain typically disappears within a few weeks or months when appropriate treatment is given. But acute pain can turn into chronic pain if the cause of the underlying pain remains untreated.

has healed, such as an infection or injury. And sometimes chronic pain has no identifiable trigger, meaning there is no prior injury or tissue damage. In this case, the cause cannot be determined, and the patient is unable to receive proper treatment and recover. In other cases, chronic pain is related to certain medical conditions, such as arthritis, low back pain, migraine, and multiple sclerosis.

Chronic pain can cause people who are normally very active to be bedridden. It can even lead to depression and suicide, particularly if the pain is really severe and relief is scarce.

How Many People Have Chronic Pain?

Chronic pain has become so *prevalent* that the Institute of Medicine referred to the situation a *crisis*. The American Pain Society reported in 2015 that nearly 50 million adults in the United States suffer from chronic pain or severe pain. As more people become afflicted with chronic pain, even more individuals—including family and friends—are affected. The total number of people directly and indirectly affected by chronic pain is therefore much higher than 50 million. Chronic pain is also a significant health concern in Canada, where one in five individuals suffered from chronic pain in 2010. The impact of chronic pain on patients, family members, and friends in Canada is similar to what such individuals in the United States experience.

To help combat the difficulties of living with chronic pain, patients are often prescribed painkillers. The problem with painkillers is that they are highly addictive and do not treat the source of the problem.

Chronic Pain and Depression

According to the Perelman School of Medicine, almost one-half of all primary care patients in America experience persistent pain. Many of these patients also suffer from major depressive disorder (MDD), which is a depressed mood that interferes with daily life. People with MDD are more likely to report chronic pain, and people with chronic pain are more likely to develop MDD. Suicide is therefore closely linked to people suffering from both conditions.

Suicidal ideation, or suicidal thoughts, may stem from being disabled or unemployed, poor sleep, and feelings of helplessness caused by chronic pain. In a study of 88 patients at several pain clinics, 24 percent reported active or passive suicidal ideation. Active suicidal ideation is the desire to die and having a specific plan for how the death will be carried out. Passive suicidal ideation is the desire to die without having a specific plan for how the death will happen.

A study of 153 individuals with chronic non-cancer pain revealed that 19 percent had passive suicidal ideation, 13 percent had active suicidal ideation, and 5 percent had a plan for suicide. In most cases, drug overdose was the chosen method for suicide.

People with chronic pain are twice as likely to commit suicide, compared to people without chronic pain. General *risk factors* include prior suicide attempts, history of suicide in the family, and depression. Pain-specific risk factors include widespread and intense pain accompanied by insomnia. Considering the high rate of depression in the pain population, doctors treating chronic pain should screen patients for depression during each visit.

How Does Addiction to Pain Medication Happen?

People who take prescription painkillers for an extensive period of time develop a tolerance for the drug, meaning they need to take more in order to feel its effects. These people become physically dependent on the painkiller, and experience painful withdrawal symptoms if they suddenly stop taking it. Physical dependence can be resolved by slowly tapering, or weaning, off the drug.

However, addiction—which is caused by taking too much of the drug—is not so easily managed. Once addicted, painkiller users have uncontrollable cravings that makes it extremely hard for them to stop using, despite the harmful consequences—which includes compulsive drug-seeking behavior and the inability to meet work, family and financial obligations. Note that most people who become addicted to painkillers were prescribed the medication to help treat their chronic pain.

Who Becomes Addicted to Pain Medication?

Addiction is not limited by age, socioeconomic class, race, ethnicity, or profession. Even celebrities can find themselves addicted to pain medication. The following are examples of a few of the many celebrities who have struggled with painkiller addiction.

Steven Tyler: Lead singer of the rock band Aerosmith and one of the judges of the television show "American Idol," Steven

Tyler has had a long and illustrious career during which he sustained a fair number of performance-related injuries. Some of these injuries required surgery, which left him in significant pain for long stretches of time. Consequently, Tyler has battled with painkiller addiction and has completed rehabilitation programs designed to treat addiction at least twice.

Steven Tyler

Matthew Perry: Known for his role as Chandler on the American television program *Friends*, Matthew Perry is an accomplished actor. After a ski accident in 1997, he was prescribed painkillers to help cope with the injury. He became addicted to the medication and attempted to deal with the issue while acting on *Friends,* one of the most popular television shows of its time.

Matthew Perry

Educational Video

Scan here to see a short video on chronic pain and related problems:

These examples show that there is no single "type" of person who becomes addicted to prescription pain medication. It can happen even to people who seem to have access to everything they could ever want. However, studies show that 50 to 80 percent of people who die from prescription opioid overdose struggled with chronic pain.

Opioid Pain Relievers

Derived from the opium poppy plant, opioid pain relievers are by far the most common form of prescription pain medication. This type of medication is used because it is very effective in

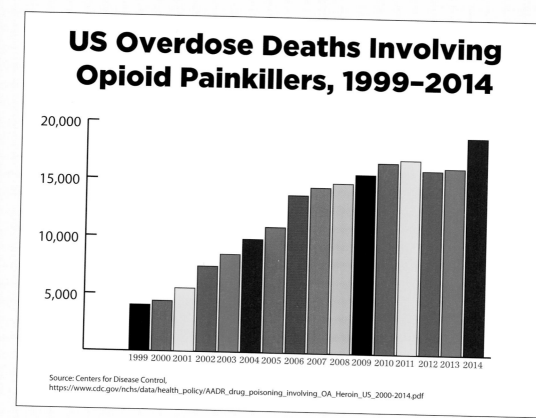

US Overdose Deaths Involving Opioid Painkillers, 1999–2014

Source: Centers for Disease Control,
https://www.cdc.gov/nchs/data/health_policy/AADR_drug_poisoning_involving_OA_Heroin_US_2000-2014.pdf

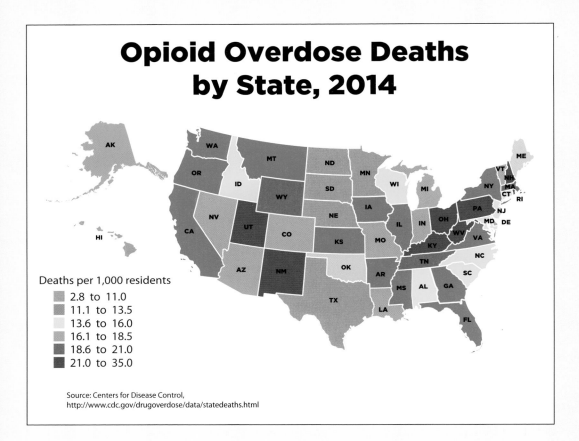

Opioid Overdose Deaths by State, 2014

Deaths per 1,000 residents

- 2.8 to 11.0
- 11.1 to 13.5
- 13.6 to 16.0
- 16.1 to 18.5
- 18.6 to 21.0
- 21.0 to 35.0

Source: Centers for Disease Control,
http://www.cdc.gov/drugoverdose/data/statedeaths.html

treating pain and relieving discomfort. It is also highly addictive and can be dangerous. According to the Centers for Disease Control and Prevention (CDC), at least half of all opioid overdoses in the United States involve a prescription opioid. And in 2014, over 14,000 deaths occurred because of prescription opioid overdose. Similarly, the number of deaths from opioid abuse in certain Canadian provinces have increased over the years. From 1991 to 2010, the opioid-related *mortality rate* in Alberta, British Columbia, and Ontario increased 242 percent. And in 2010, opioids were the cause of death for 12.1 percent of Ontario individuals aged 25 to 34.

Despite the rising number of addicts and deaths directly linked to opioid pain relievers, these drugs continue to be routinely prescribed to people with chronic pain. The pharmaceutical industry makes billions of dollars each year from prescription opioids, such as oxycodone and hydrocodone. In 2013, more than 206 million prescriptions for opioid pain relievers were filled in the United States. In Canada, 18.3 million opioid prescriptions were dispensed in 2012, and in 2014, that amount jumped to 21.7 million. As health conditions—such as diseases and catastrophic injuries—persist, the issues of chronic pain and prescription painkiller abuse continue to escalate.

 Text-Dependent Questions

1. How many people in the United States suffer from chronic pain?
2. Has the prevalence of opioid-related mortality increased or decreased in Canada?
3. Where do most addicts obtain the pain medication that they abuse?

Research Project

How is chronic pain and opioid addiction affecting your state or province? Look up statistics relating to both of these issues and write a one-page summary explaining the impact on your region.

Words to Understand in This Chapter

compliance—refers to the act of obeying or conforming, such as acting "in compliance" with the law.

perpetuate—to cause something to keep happening.

synthesize—refers to chemical synthesis, which is the process of combining different chemicals to make a whole.

vested interest—when someone wants something to happen in a certain way because it will benefit them.

Today, a drug called Fentanyl is one of the most widely used opioids. It is prescribed both as a painkiller and as a anesthetic. Although the drug is safe when dosages are monitored carefully in a medical setting, Fentanyl has also proven to be popular among recreational drug users. However, the drug is 40 to 50 times stronger than heroin, and overdoses among casual users are tragically common.

The Evolution of Opioid Painkillers

To understand the development of opioid painkillers, it is necessary to examine the beginning stages of opioids. Around the third millennium BCE, the Sumerians—who lived in what is called Iraq today—grew poppy plants that contained opium. The Sumerians separated opium from their seed capsules and named opium "gil," which means joy. They called the poppy plant "hul gil," which means plant of joy. Initially, opium was used in religious rituals for its euphoric effects, and was taken orally or by inhaling it from heated vessels.

Opium was also used medicinally, in combination with the poisonous hemlock plant, to put people swiftly and painlessly to death. Various opium remedies were used as pain relievers, but physicians remained cautious of them because they all had

17

different levels of potency. In addition, opium abuse and addiction was becoming rampant, particularly in China—where the practice of smoking opium started in the mid-17th century, after tobacco smoking was outlawed.

Opioid Production in the Early Years

In the early 1800s, the active ingredient in opium was separated and named morphine, after Morpheus, the god of dreams. After the invention of the hypodermic needle in the 1850s,

An Afghan farmer holds the seed pod of an opium poppy. Juice from the seed pod can be refined into pain-killing opiates like morphine and codeine. A separate class of drugs, called opioids, are synthetic compounds that mimic the effects of opiates. These drugs include substances that are currently illegal in the United States because they have no medicinal value, such as heroin, as well as drugs that are prescribed as painkillers such as hydrocodone and oxycodone.

morphine was used for chronic pain, in surgical procedures, and in combination with other general sedatives. But, like opium, morphine had a high potential for abuse, and was not very safe to use. As a result, pain researchers spent a lot of time trying to develop a safer, more effective, non-addicting opiate. Heroin was *synthesized* in the late 1800s, and was said to be stronger and less addicting than morphine. Mass production of heroin stopped in the early 1900s, when the drug was found to be harmful and addicting.

Near the mid-1900s, methadone was synthesized. Methadone's pharmacological properties are similar to morphine, but it is also slower acting, less intense, and lasts longer than morphine. Health care providers typically give methadone to opiate addicts, as an alternative to morphine. A few years after heroin production stopped, oxycodone was synthesized with the hope that it would keep the sedative effects of morphine and heroin without being addicting. But due to their high potential for abuse, addiction and overdose, opioids in general were usually prescribed only to cancer patients and people experiencing excruciating pain.

The Big Pharma Crisis

By the 1990s, pain societies began encouraging doctors to push for the increased use of opioids for all types of pain, including non-cancer pain. According to the American Association of Retired Persons, this push for more extensive use of painkillers was largely financed by pharmaceutical companies who had a *vested interest* in making a profit. The drug makers greatly downplayed the medications' potential for addiction while exaggerating their effectiveness. As a result, physicians had the impression that prescription painkillers were much safer and more effective for chronic pain than they truly were.

Between 1996 and 2002, Purdue Pharma, the manufacturer of OxyContin (oxycodone), financed over 20,000 educational programs for physicians. Many of these programs endorsed the long-term use of opioids for chronic pain. The campaigns were successful. Over the next 15 years, opioid pain reliever use in the United States doubled and oxycodone use grew almost fivefold. However, researchers found hardly any evidence to support the claim that long-term opioid use helps. Instead, they discovered overwhelming evidence pointing to the potential for abuse, addiction, overdose, falls, fractures, constipation, sexual dysfunction, and heart attacks.

OxyContin began as a drug for relieving serious pain associated with cancer. But Purdue's heavy marketing of the drug soon resulted in people across North America using it for all types of pain, including toothaches and back pain. According to the Council of Canadians, Purdue's misleading statements to doctors about OxyContin's effectiveness and safeness has triggered a public health epidemic that claims the lives of around

 ## Educational Video

Scan here to see a video history of how opioids became a national epidemic:

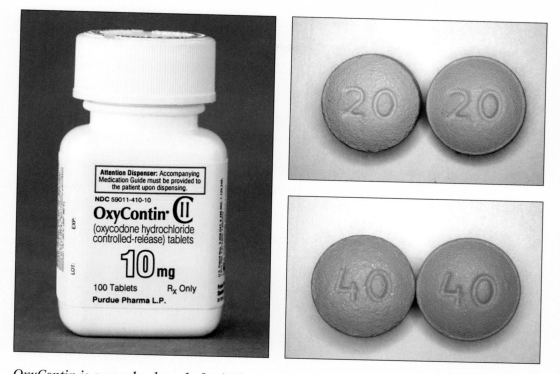

OxyContin is a popular brand of opioid painkiller in which the drug is slowly released into the person's system over a twelve-hour period. It comes in strengths of 10 to 80 miligrams; pictured (above, right) are 20 and 40 miligram doses.

30,000 North Americans each year. Purdue Pharma pleaded guilty to criminal charges and agreed to pay over $600 million in fines and other payments for misbranding its product.

The Role of Pharmacies in the Opioid Epidemic

Pharmacies face major obstacles in cracking down on the misuse and abuse of prescription painkillers. The problem for pharmacists is twofold: detect drug abusers and refuse to fill their prescription, and supply medication to legitimate patients who are really in pain. It is not always easy for pharmacists to know whether someone is buying pain medication for legitimate reasons. The U.S. Drug Enforcement Administration (DEA) has identified specific warning signs that pharmacists can use to determine whether or not to fill a prescription. For example, drug abusers tend to pay with cash to avoid being detected based on health insurance. But situations vary, so red flags do not always mean that someone is misusing prescription drugs.

Although many pharmacies take sincere measures to pre-

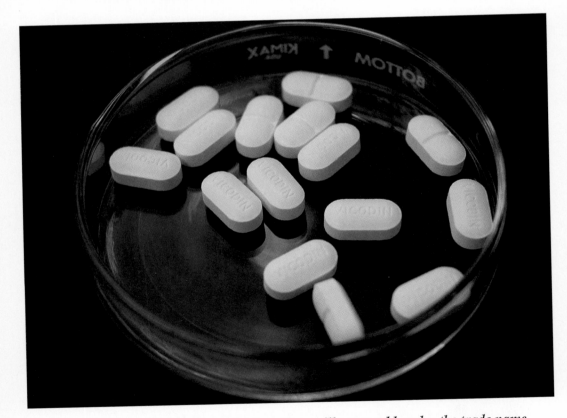

Hydrocodone is an opioid pain medication. These pills were sold under the trade name Vicodin.

Did You Know?

The Federation of State Medical Boards, American Academy of Pain Medicine, Joint Commission, and American Pain Society received financial support from Purdue Pharma for encouraging the use of opioid painkillers. In addition, the American Geriatrics Society modified its guidelines in 2009 to recommend opioid therapy for all patients with moderate to severe pain.

vent prescription painkiller abuse, there are some unethical ones who illegally dispense prescription painkillers just to make a profit. In Kentucky, a pharmacist was sentenced to 54 months in prison for filling prescriptions he knew were false. The evidence revealed that he dispensed hydrocodone and oxycodone prescribed by physicians who did not exist. He also filled prescriptions written by several disreputable doctors, knowing they were not for legitimate uses.

Some drug dealers and unethical pharmacists take their business online. The National Association of Boards of Pharmacy (NABP) has reviewed more than 11,000 online drug outlets that sell prescription medications, and 96 percent of them have been classified as "Not Recommended" because they are not in *compliance* with the law and pharmacy industry standards.

Pill Mills and Untrained Physicians

Most abusers obtain painkillers via a prescription. Studies

Signs of a Pill Mill

There are many indicators that a clinic or doctor may be running a pill mill. The most telling sign is doctors who prescribe or dispense painkillers without performing or requiring a physical exam. This is a huge red flag because physicians should evaluate patients' physical condition before prescribing powerful medications.

Another warning sign is doctors who accept only cash as payment and/or treat pain only with prescription medication, without providing any other options. Doctors such as these usually do not care about their patients' well-being and are only interested in making quick money.

A doctor running a pill mill may meet up with multiple patients in parking lots. Similar to drug dealing activity, there may be excessive traffic coming in and out of the doctor's office. These patients tend to enter and leave the office quickly, within a matter of minutes, because they are there simply to get a prescription or buy more painkillers. Neighboring business owners may complain about the clientele visiting the clinic or doctor's office, and pharmacists may complain about the doctor's practices. Pill mill doctors also usually make large cash deposits at banks.

Although it is hard to spot some of these warning signs, there are ways to do so. For example, complaints about the clientele can be overheard from inside the doctor's office or outside of the building.

These indicators by themselves do not necessarily mean that the doctor is running a pill mill. A legitimate small office, for example, may accept only cash at certain times. Therefore, look for multiple signs, based on the clientele and physician's actions.

show that 18 percent of people who abuse prescription painkillers got them from the same physician. And another 54.2 percent received the painkillers for free from a relative or friend—who obtained the drugs from a single physician in 81.6 percent of all cases. Abusers use various methods to escape detection, such as "doctor shopping," in which they obtain prescriptions from different doctors to get large amounts or regular refills of the drug. Although most physicians prescribe painkillers in a genuine attempt to prevent abuse and addiction, a few "bad apples"—called rogue physicians—vastly contribute to the problem.

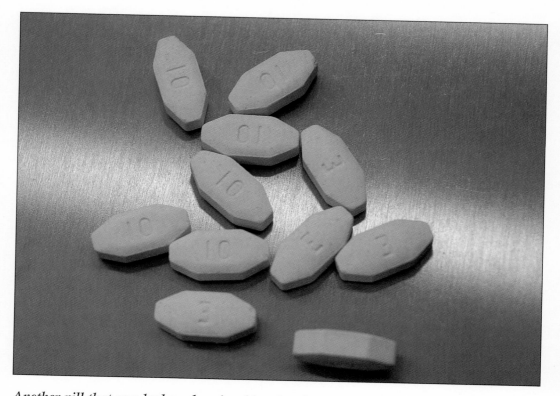

Another pill that uses hydrocodone is sold under the trade name Zydone, and is prescribed to treat back pain, pain and rheumatoid arthritis.

Newspaper headlines announce the death of the pop star Prince in April 2016. The talented musician overdosed on fentanyl, an opioid painkiller that he had been prescribed as treatment for a hip injury.

In 2005, former Houston doctor Callie Hall Herpin sold over 17,000 opioid prescriptions for $1.7 million in cash. Herpin, who pleaded guilty to the charges, sold the narcotics to drug dealers and other buyers who filled the prescriptions with the help of rogue pharmacists. Some physicians dispense the drugs illegally themselves. As explained by the *American Journal of Law and Medicine*, doctors have strong financial reasons for supplying prescription painkillers out of their office. They can buy opioids wholesale, repackage them, and sell them to patients at a much higher price, with profits ranging from 60 to 300 percent. These illegal operations in which doctors, clinics or pharmacies prescribe or supply opioids without a legitimate medical reason are called "pill mills."

The opioid epidemic is also *perpetuated* by physicians who, despite having the best of intentions, lack the training needed to appropriately prescribe controlled substances. According to the *American Journal of Law and Medicine*, 44 percent of physicians report having no medical training in prescribing controlled substances. And 60 percent said that they did not receive any guidance in medical school on spotting prescription drug abuse and addiction.

 Text-Dependent Questions

1. What types of pain were opioids initially prescribed for?
2. How did the pharmaceutical industry contribute to the opioid epidemic?
3. What difficulties do pharmacists face when presented with prescriptions for painkillers?

Research Project

Write down the number of doctors listed in the DEA's "Cases Against Doctors" (http://www.deadiversion.usdoj.gov/crim_admin_actions/doctors_criminal_cases.pdf). Figure the number of reported arrests for each year by breaking down the "Date of Arrest" data into years. Present the results to your class.

Words to Understand in This Chapter

best practices—a set of guidelines, rules, ideas, or ethics that are accepted or regarded as the most accurate or effective.

conflicting—a state of opposition, disharmony, disagreement or contradiction over something, such as ideas or beliefs.

poly-drug users—people who combine and take two or more drugs to achieve a specific effect. Poly-drug abuse is a dangerous practice that can be fatal.

Police officers in Phoenix, Arizona, collect unwanted prescription drugs as part of the "National Prescription Drug Take-Back Day" sponsored by the federal Drug Enforcement Administration (DEA). Since the program began in 2010, more than 7 million pounds of prescription drugs have been collected.

3

Controlling the Epidemic

The United States comprises only 4.6 percent of the world's population, but consumes 81 percent of the oxycodone supplied in the world. Consequently, the issue of prescription painkiller abuse is most prevalent in the United States. The National Safety Council reported in 2016 that 1.9 million Americans are addicted to opioid pain medication, and 4.3 million adults and adolescents reported using prescription opioids non-medically in 2014.

Overall, the numbers are lower in Canada. In 2015, around 2 percent of people who used opioid pain relievers in Canada reported abusing them. Prescription opioid abuse is a growing concern in Canada, despite the lower statistics. And in the United States, the problem has gotten so widespread that law-

29

makers are pushing for stricter policies aimed at controlling the epidemic.

The Crackdown on Pill Mills

To combat prescription opioid abuse, the DEA and some states have taken steps to eradicate pill mills. The issue of unethical pain clinics was particularly rampant in the state of Florida, which had over 1,000 pain clinics during the mid to late 2000s. These clinics were cash-only businesses, where providers did not perform proper, if any, physical exams before prescribing or dispensing significant amounts of opioids, often in conjunction with benzodiazepines—which are mainly used to treat anxiety.

In 2010 and 2011, Florida passed laws that made it difficult for pill mills to supply pain medication at their locations. Law enforcement officers in Florida also began to actively search for, arrest and prosecute people operating pill mills in the state. Since 2010, Florida has experienced a substantial decline in the number of physicians who buy oxycodone and prescribe opioids plus in the amount of people who purchase prescription

Did You Know?

Nearly 50 percent of teens in the United States believe that prescription drugs are much safer than illicit street drugs. In addition, one out of eight high school seniors report using prescription opioids for non-medical purposes. And seven out of 10 non-medical users reported mixing prescription drugs with alcohol and/or at least one other drug in the past year—which puts them at a substantial risk for overdose.

medication for someone else. To keep a lid on the problem, Florida uses databases to monitor what physicians are prescribing. Other states, such as New York and Massachusetts, have joined the fight against pill mills.

In 2015, the DEA carried out raids at pharmacies, pain clinics and other areas in the South, including Arkansas, Louisiana, Mississippi, and Alabama. The raid targeted the illegal sale of painkillers, including oxycodone and hydrocodone. Although state and DEA efforts seem to be paying off, there is some debate regarding opioid painkiller users transitioning to heroin or buying pain medication from unsafe pharmacies online.

Heroin Use in Prescription Drug Abusers

Because opioid painkillers are structured similarly to heroin, they provide similar effects to heroin on the mind and body. For this reason, the association between prescription opioid abuse and increases in heroin use is being examined in the United States. According to the National Safety Council, over 900,000 people reported using heroin in 2014, an increase of 153 percent since 2007. Heroin-related deaths have tripled from 2010 to 2014, going from 3,300 to over 10,000 deaths. A study revealed that out of 600 heroin users, four out five said that they began with opioid painkillers. And people using opioids for non-medical reasons were 19 times more likely to use heroin than people who do not misuse opioids.

Interestingly, the National Institute on Drug Abuse (NIDA) stated that although prescription opioid abuse is an increasing risk factor in heroin use, only a small number of

Many states have turned to tougher licensing restrictions in order to crack down on the "pill mill" clinics that fueled the current opioid crisis.

painkiller abusers transition to heroin. Based on general population data, less than 4 percent of people who abused prescription painkillers began using heroin within five years. The estimated 4 percent tends to be *poly-drug users* and the switch to heroin may be a natural thing for them.

There is *conflicting* data as to whether pill mill crackdowns contributed to the increase in heroin use. For example, one study concluded that the Florida pill mill crackdown is working and did not encourage prescription opioid abusers to start using heroin. But other reports argue that shutting down pill mills have caused a drastic pill shortage, causing painkiller abusers to seek out heroin—which is cheaper and easier to obtain than prescription opioids. Regardless of whether the crackdown on pill mills contributed to the increase in heroin use, it is clear that heroin addiction is an epidemic.

Heroin addiction has gotten so out of control that Canada has developed a controversial treatment plan that legalizes prescription heroin. The program allows addicts to access heroin in a legal and safe environment so they do not have to resort to committing crimes to obtain the drug. Once enrolled in the program, addicts are offered or forcibly placed into rehabilitation.

Websites Selling Illegal Drugs

Pharmacy websites classified as "Not Recommended" by the NABP are fueling the opioid epidemic. These unsafe drug outlets make it easy for opiate addicts to buy prescription medicines illegally online, without a valid prescription. But consumers face considerable dangers when buying drugs from unapproved Internet sources because the product may contain hidden, deadly ingredients. Getting rid of these unsafe websites has proven difficult for the NABP because as soon as the organization detects them, more appear. The NABP's list of "Recommended" and "Not Recommended" online pharmacies can be found on the organization's website.

Reduction Efforts of the Federal Government

Prescription drug abuse comes with substantial economic consequences. One study shows that prescription drug abuse causes over $72 billion in medical costs each year in the United

States. Other research shows the cost to be between $53 and $56 billion annually, which include medical and treatment costs, criminal justice costs, and loss work productivity.

The U.S. federal government has created a number of strategies to curb the cost of prescription drug abuse and the rising rate of opioid addiction and related deaths. Strategies include using surveillance data to track prescription drug abuse, identifying which populations are at risk for abuse, and

Canada's Response to the Crisis

In an effort to lower the opioid overdose rate, Purdue Pharma removed the controversial drug OxyContin from the Canadian market in 2012. The drug manufacturer replaced OxyContin with a different drug, OxyNEO, which is harder to crush and more unlikely to be abused through snorting or injecting. However, some doctors argue that because OxyNEO has the same sedative properties as OxyContin, it can be abused by taking heavy doses orally.

To combat prescription opioid abuse, the Canadian government expanded its National Anti-Drug Strategy to include prescription drug abuse. The plan is supported by a budget of more than $44 million for over five years, with the key strategy being developing partnerships and collaborating directly with stakeholders. This engagement strategy involves discussions among provincial officers, physicians, pharmacists, law enforcement, addiction specialists, and other industry leaders to find solutions to prescription drug abuse. The National Anti-Drug Strategy for prescription drug abuse also focuses on strategies for keeping communities healthy and safe, such as promoting appropriate use of opioid pain medications.

Educational Video

To see a video of drug enforcement agents arresting a pill mill doctor, scan here:

detecting emerging prescription drug abuse trends. Other strategies include identifying areas in the health care system that needs to change and the impact of those changes, and assisting with legislative decision making.

The federal government also aims to evaluate the effectiveness of drug abuse prevention programs; perform social science research to understand the process of prescription drug abuse; and evaluate the efficiency of medical disposal programs—which promote safe practices for disposing of medications.

The Role of NASPER and Federal Grants

The National All Schedules Prescription Electronic Reporting Act of 2005 (NASPER) is a U.S. federal law that consists of two objectives: (1) help develop state-operated prescription drug monitoring programs (PDMPs); and (2) establish *best practices* for new and existing PDMPs. Prescription drug monitoring programs are electronic databases that monitor the distribution of prescription drugs. A prescriber can look up a patient's profile in his or her state's PDMP and see if there

A block of Fentanyl seized in a DEA raid. Because Fentanyl causes effects similar to heroin, the two drugs are sometimes mixed when sold illegally in order to increase the potency of low-grade heroin. However, including too much Fentanyl in the mix can lead to a deadly overdose, as the drug is roughly 100 times more powerful than heroin.

have been any inappropriate prescribing patterns in the patient's history.

Besides offering an information tool for physicians to prescribe medications and identify illicit drug use and abuse, NASPER provides grants to states with PDMPs. However, no state funding has occurred through NASPER since fiscal year 2010. Since then, the Department of Human Health Services and the Office of National Coordinator has given grants to certain states for preliminary small-scale PDMP projects. Furthermore, in 2016, the White House announced President Obama's proposal for $1.1 billion in new funding to help opioid abusers get the help they need.

Because federal grant programs usually limit the amount that states can receive, the funding period, and how funds should be spent, states are forced to compete for awards. The most successful state applications are those that comply with the federal grant requirements, capably show the need for funding, and clearly demonstrate PDMP goals and ability to meet them. Some states partner with grant writing specialists or research institutions to increase their chances of securing federal grants.

 Text-Dependent Questions

1. What methods are states and the DEA using to crack down on pill mills?
2. How can consumers tell whether an online prescription drug outlet is recommended or not recommended?
3. How can states obtain funding for their PDMP from the federal government?

Research Project

Read the Obama administration's proposal for addressing prescription opioid abuse and the heroin epidemic (https://www.whitehouse.gov/the-press-office/2016/03/29/fact-sheet-obama-administration-announces-additional-actions-address). Write a report on the federal agencies that have agreed to provide funding opportunities, the funding amounts, and what each amount will cover.

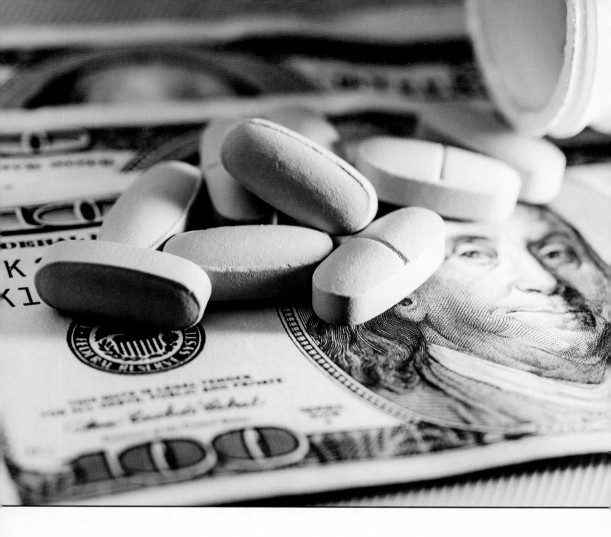

 Words to Understand in This Chapter

anti-inflammatories—medications, like aspirin, that reduce signs of inflammation—such as pain, swelling, and tenderness.

diversion—when prescription drugs are unlawfully used or obtained. As in "drug" diversion.

musculoskeletal injury—disorders or injuries that affect movement of the human body.

paraphernalia—equipment needed for a certain task or activity.

4

Some unscrupulous doctors prescribe painkillers without medical justification. These "pill mills" become a way to enrich the doctor, without regard for those whose health or lives may suffer as a consequence of using opioids.

Physician and Local Enforcement Challenge

The prescription opioid epidemic has far-reaching effects, not only on a federal level but also on a state or provincial level. As states, provinces, physicians and local law enforcement look for ways to prevent prescription abuse and overdose, they are finding that the issue is very complex.

Physicians Struggle to Find Balance

Physicians are under intense pressure when it comes to prescribing opioids for patients dealing with chronic pain. The threat of legal sanctions, or penalties, continues to influence physicians' decision to prescribe (or to not prescribe) opioid medications, and the dosage amount if prescribed. These sanc-

tions include the removal of a physician's prescribing capabilities, loss of medical license, and even criminal charges.

Physicians rely on a mix of subjective and objective evidence to assess the risks versus benefits of prescribing opioids to patients. Subjective evidence refers to the patient's perception of his or her medical condition. Objective evidence is the physician's observations of the patient's condition. Ideally, the complaints of the patient should be consistent with what the physician sees for himself or herself.

For example, a patient who complains of lower back pain may have an X-ray performed which shows a *musculoskeletal injury* that is consistent with the patient's complaint. The physician must then decide whether an opioid is the right medication to prescribe for this patient. And if so, what dose and for how long. Pain patients are normally asked to rate the severity of their pain on a numeric scale of 0 to 10—with 10 being the most severe pain, and 0 being no pain is experienced. This rating process helps physicians understand the pain the patient is experiencing and whether prescribing opioids is the best course of action.

Recommended Actions

Before deciding to prescribe opioids, physicians should screen patients thoroughly to see whether they are at risk for opioid abuse. There are many factors in a patient's history that can alert the physician as to whether the patient is at risk. This includes having a psychiatric history, showing a pattern of drug or alcohol abuse, and being unwilling to try non-opioid alternatives to pain management. To effectively manage chronic pain, physicians and their patients must develop a trusting relationship that seeks to achieve pain management goals.

In 2016, the CDC released guidelines for physicians to use when treating chronic pain unrelated to cancer or end-of-life care. The guidelines discourage prescribing opioids routinely and instead favors non-opioids, such as *anti-inflammatories*, used in combination with non-medicinal therapies, such as exercise. The CDC suggests that if opiates are to be prescribed, the dosage should be low enough to be effective and used for a short period of time. Although the CDC provides wise recommendations for physicians, the guidelines are not legally bind-

US Drug Schedules

In the United States, drugs are placed into five categories, known as schedules, to help identify risk of abuse and dependency as well as suggested medical use, if any, for the drug. Schedule 1 drugs, such as ecstasy, heroin and LSD, are considered the most dangerous drugs of all. These drugs have a high potential for abuse and are not accepted for medical use. Schedule II drugs include cocaine, oxycodone, fentanyl, methadone and Adderall, which all carry a high potential for abuse and can cause serious physical or psychological dependence.

Schedule III drugs include ketamine and Tylenol with codeine, which have a moderate to low potential for physical and psychological dependence. Schedule IV drugs, such as Tramadol, Xanax, Valium and Ambien, have a low potential for abuse and dependency. Schedule V drugs, such as cough syrups with under 200 milligrams of codeine, contain limited amounts of specific narcotics and have the lowest potential for abuse.

ing, leaving the monitoring of poor prescribing practices to the government.

Limitations on Physicians

Several states and provinces have passed laws that mandate dosage and time thresholds that further limit a physician's prescribing power. In the state of Washington, physicians are required to consult with a board-certified pain specialist before prescribing daily doses of opioids equivalent to 120 milligrams or more of morphine. The physician may not have to consult with the pain specialist if he or she has completed continuing education hours about chronic pain management. Each state and province has their own time limit that controls the amount of the opioid supplied at one time. In twenty-three states, Schedule II opioids, like fentanyl and oxycodone, are limited to a 30-day supply. And Massachusetts has passed a law that limits first-time opioid prescriptions to seven days of use, with the exception being cancer patients and people suffering from chronic pain.

Guidelines and standards from high authorities like the CDC and the state government have led to a more cautious attitude among physicians in regards to how they prescribe opioid medications. However, research shows that chronic pain is often undertreated and physicians' fear of legal sanctions has been proposed to be a factor in this finding.

State PDMPs under Criticism

As of 2016, 49 states have a PDMP, but the biggest criticism of PDMPs is that they are not all alike. For example, some states require physicians to check the patient's prescription history in the PDMP while other states do not. And because PDMPs are established and ran by the state government, there can be a lack of information sharing among state PDMPs. For example, a physician in Tennessee may not be aware that an opioid-seeking patient just received opioids a week ago in Alabama. There are also concerns over whether all prescription medications are actually reported to the PDMP.

PDMPs are not meant to be an enforcement tool. They are intended to be a resource that the health care team—including physicians and pharmacists—can use to collaborate and prevent opioid misuse, abuse and *diversion*.

Law Enforcement Attitudes and Perceptions

Death by opioid overdose is preventable if the patient is tended to in time. As the first responders in many opioid overdose incidents, police officers are often equipped with naloxone (or Narcan), a medication that reverses the deadly effects of opioids. With police officers having access to Narcan, life saving measures for the overdosed individual can occur without help from paramedics.

 ## Educational Video

Scan here for a short video on how communities are responding to the opioid epidemic:

Did You Know?

Naloxone (Narcan) can reverse effects of opioid overdose within five minutes of injection. The drug, created in the 1960's, is on the World Health Organization's list of essential medications and is considered one the most important medications in the world.

With an already stressful job, police officers struggle to deal with the additional burden of preventing and treating overdoses in their communities. A 2013 study exploring the attitudes of law enforcement toward overdose prevention found that many police officers felt criminal arrest was the most effective thing they could do for opioid addicts. They complained that counseling drug addicts was not helpful due to the lack of accessible treatment resources for opioid addicts—especially the poorer ones who already have social and financial challenges.

Some precinct officers believe that Narcan should applied only by individuals with a trained medical background, instead of by police officers. In certain states and provinces, Narcan is available to opiate addicts, as well as to their peers and family members in case they happen to be around during the overdose. Expanding the availability of Narcan is a controversial subject, which is commonly discussed among local communities battling the opioid epidemic.

Good Samaritan Laws

Bystanders or eyewitnesses to opioid overdose may delay call-

State Legislation: Overdose Prevention

States with Overdose Good Samaritan Laws

States with Naloxone Access Laws

States with both Overdose Good Samaritan and Naloxone Access Laws

Source: Drug Policy Alliance, http://www.drugpolicy.org/resource/which-states-have-911-good-samaritan-laws-andor-naloxone-access-laws

ing, or simply not call, emergency services out of fear of being arrested in relation to the overdose. In many states, Good Samaritan laws have been put in place to combat this particular fear of police involvement. These laws protect eyewitnesses from arrest or prosecution as long as the issues surrounding the scene at the time is simple drug possession, possession of *paraphernalia* used for drugs, and being under the influence

Pallets of containers containing prescription drugs collected, and subsequently destroyed, after a DEA-sponsored National Take-Back Day event.

of drugs. Not all states and provinces have Good Samaritan laws that provide protection to eyewitnesses. However, lawmakers have proposed that such laws should be consistent nationwide in both the United States and Canada.

Drug Take-Back Day

Law enforcement agencies have set up Drug Take-Back days that allow the public to safely and anonymously discard medications, at no charge, no questions asked. These medications are often unused, unwanted, or expired. The program encourages individuals to dispose of their medications safely, while allowing law enforcement personnel to educate the public on opioid misuse, abuse and diversion. There is also an environmental benefit: medications are not being flushed down the toilet, which is a common way of discarding medications and has a damaging impact on the public's water.

 Text-Dependent Questions

1. What patient factors can influence a physician's decisions in relation to prescribing opioid medications?
2. What are the challenges of PDMPs?
3. How are police officers helping to prevent overdoses in their communities?

 Research Project

Research whether your state or province has a prescription drug monitoring program. Write a one-page summary of rules surrounding the program—such as who manages the program, who can access the program, and the information that the program provides. If your state or province does not have a PDMP, share your beliefs in support or against the creation of a PDMP in your area.

 Words to Understand in This Chapter

opioid agonist—a drug that mimics the effects of opiates by attaching to the opioid receptors in the brain.

opioid antagonist—a drug that blocks opioids by attaching to the opioid receptors without acting on them, causing no opioid effect.

pathophysiological—the biological processes and mechanisms in the body that cause the signs and symptoms of a disease or abnormal state.

regimen—a strict plan or program (such as exercise, diet, or treatment) designed to produce good results.

5

Recommended Use, Alternatives, and Addiction Treatment

As discussed, prescription painkillers have a high potential for abuse, but can be very effective in relieving chronic pain. Issues with abuse, addiction, and overdose generally stem from taking too many prescription painkillers, taking them too often, or consuming them with illegal drugs, alcohol or incompatible medicines. Therefore, prescription painkillers should be taken only as prescribed, and for legitimate health reasons, such as to relieve chronic pain from surgery or an illness.

Tips for Safe Use

Upon getting their prescription filled, patients should check the label to ensure that it is the appropriate medication. If a measuring device is included in the prescription, instructions

for using the tool should be followed precisely. Patients should never change the prescribed dosage without consulting their doctor first. They should also avoid taking medication prescribed for someone else—this is especially important because the dose that is safe for the prescribed user may be deadly for someone else.

Before consuming prescription painkillers, patients should ask their doctor about the side effects and for any precautionary measures that they can take. For example, opioid use can cause drowsiness, so upon taking the medication, it is best not to drive or use any equipment that may cause injury. Patients taking other medicines or dietary supplements should tell their doctor before they start using prescription painkillers. They should also inform their physician if they are becoming dependent on or addicted to the drug.

Spotting Overmedication and Overdose

Taking too many opiates can cause overmedication or overdose. Signs of overmedication include dizziness, confusion, slurred speech, stumbling while walking, extreme drowsiness,

 Educational Video

For some information about treatment for opiate addiction, scan here:

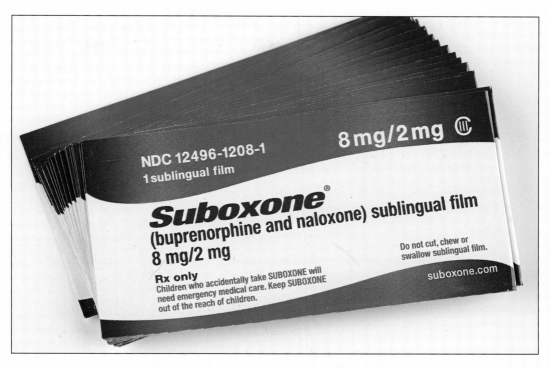

Suboxone combines buprenorphine, a long-acting narcotic, and naloxone, an opiate antago-nist administered sublingualy to treat narcotics additions in long-term programs.

problems staying focused, and difficulty waking from sleep. Signs of overdose include inability to stay awake or speak; breathing problems such as slow, shallow breathing; lifeless-ness or limpness; blue fingernails or lips; clammy or pale skin; and stopped heartbeat. Addicts and their family and friends should learn the signs of overmedication and overdose so they know how to respond in such situations.

Alternative Medications

Patients experiencing pain should receive whichever treatment delivers the most benefit. Depending on the medical condition, non-opioid alternatives—which include non-opioid medications and non-pharmacological therapies—may be ideal. According to the CDC, non-opioid medications include acetaminophen, non-steroidal anti-inflammatory drugs (NSAIDs), gabapentin/pregabalin, tricyclic antidepressants (TCAs), serotonin/norepinephrine reuptake inhibitors (SNRIs), and topical agents such as lidocaine and NSAIDs. These medications are generally safer than opioids, but they carry side effects nonetheless and should be used with caution.

The CDC also provides recommendations for non-opioid medications, based on common chronic pain conditions. For example, acetaminophen and NSAIDs are primary treatments for low back pain; secondary treatments include TCAs and SNRIs. Beta blockers, anti-seizure medications, and TCAs can be used to prevent migraines; and acetaminophen, aspirin, and NSAIDs may be appropriate for acute care. Topical lidocaine, TCAs, and gabapentin/pregabalin are recommended for neuropathic pain, which is pain resulting from injury to the nervous system.

Non-pharmacological Alternatives

Research conducted by the Canadian Agency for Drugs and Technologies in Health reveals various non-pharmacological pain management treatments, including relaxation, physical activity or exercise, mindfulness-based therapies such as cognitive behavioral therapy, manual therapies such as massage and physical therapy, and acupuncture. Based on CDC guidelines, patients with low back pain should limit bed-rest and stay active. People with osteoarthritis can engage in exercise and weight loss. For pain associated with fibromyalgia, the CDC suggests cognitive behavioral therapy and low-impact exercise such as brisk walking or bicycling.

Non-pharmacological treatments are potentially effective for pain management in the intensive care unit (ICU). These treatments are normally inexpensive, easy to administer, and safe; health care providers can usually implement them with few problems. In ICU settings, non-pharmacological treatments are generally used alongside pharmacological treatment.

Quitting Prescription Painkillers

The American Academy of Pain Medicine states that the people most likely to become dependent on prescription painkillers are those who take prescription painkillers continuously, have a previous history of substance abuse, and are less accepting of pain. Those dependent on or addicted to opioid painkillers, such as OxyContin and hydrocodone, find it difficult to stop taking the drug even if they want to, due to extreme withdrawal. Symptoms of withdrawal include nausea, vomiting, muscle cramping, agitation, depression, anxiety, chills and goose bumps, diarrhea, body aches, and opiate cravings. Due to the severity of these symptoms, addicts are advised to seek professional guidance when quitting opiates.

Pharmacological Treatments for Opioid Addiction

The three most common medications used to treat prescription opioid addiction are naltrexone, methadone, and buprenorphine. The *opioid antagonist* naltrexone works by stopping

Methadone Side Effects

Methadone emerged during the 1950s as a treatment for opioid addiction and has remained the main therapy for this condition since then. Although methadone is structured differently from other opiates, it contains significant painkilling effects—which has been used to manage chronic pain, including cancer pain. Methadone's unique pharmacological structure allows it to act as a treatment for opioid addiction and as a pain reliever, but it has possible side effects that physicians and users should be aware of.

The side effects of methadone—which are similar to those of other opioid agonists—include nausea, itching, constipation, drowsiness, slow breathing, and irregular heartbeat. When taken orally, methadone can cause excess sweating and flushing of the face. Doctors should use caution when putting patients on methadone and increasing doses because it can take two to five days for severe side effects to show up.

Combining methadone with alcohol or other drugs can increase the side effects of sleepiness and inadequate breathing. For example, an Australian study found that benzodiazepines was present in 74 percent of methadone-related deaths. Also, people who take methadone regularly develop physical dependency on the drug and experience withdrawal symptoms once they stop taking it.

opiates from acting on the brain. It removes the reward of getting high on opiates, making it very effective in preventing relapses. Naltrexone may not stop drug cravings, so addicts might need to speak with their health care provider about other ways of reducing opiate cravings.

Methadone, a synthetic *opioid agonist*, eliminates opiate cravings and withdrawal symptoms by imitating the effects of opiates. Because methadone blocks the effects of heroin, oxycodone and other opiates, the user will not get high off those drugs if he or she relapses. Methadone does not cure opiate addiction. Instead, it stops the addict from going into withdrawal so he or she can avoid using opiates and begin the road to recovery.

Buprenorphine suppresses opiate withdrawal symptoms and cravings. Unlike methadone, which is a full agonist, buprenorphine is a partial agonist, meaning it has both agonist and antagonist properties.

Pharmacological treatments for addiction have side effects in some people, and should be used carefully, under the supervision of a physician.

Therapy Can Help

For many addicts, medication is only half of their treatment *regimen*, with therapy being the other half. Therapy allows the

 Did You Know?

Opioid treatment centers (OTPs) in the United States offer medically-assisted treatment (MAT) to people who misuse and abuse opioids. Patients undergoing treatment at OTPs must receive medical, counseling, educational, vocational and other evaluations and treatment services. As of 2015, nearly every state had OTPs in operation, with the exception being North Dakota and Wyoming.

addict to interact with a professional in a one-on-one setting or in a group environment with others who are also in treatment. Through therapy, the addict learns the reasons behind his or her addiction; that is, what motivated him or her to use and abuse drugs. Therapy encourages addicts to stick with the treatment program, and teaches them how commit to a healthier lifestyle such as by forming friendships with people who do not use drugs.

Future Opportunities

Throughout the last few decades, there has been considerable advancement in the identification, understanding, acknowledgement, and management of chronic pain. There is increased understanding of the *pathophysiological* processes of pain, more focus on holistic care, expansion of training programs on pain management, and increasing awareness at the national and international level. Despite this progress, patients with chronic pain are still lacking the help they need in regards to pain education and accessing specialist services plus effective treatments. Specialist and primary care physicians, national policy makers, researchers, and pharmaceutical companies all have a part to play in addressing these needs. For example, the pharmaceutical industry's role is to develop competent new therapies for tackling chronic pain and to engage in ethical marketing practices.

Because prescription painkillers are effective when used properly and are widely marketed, it is difficult to successfully convey that they are damaging when abused. Consequently, there is a need for more research that provides communication strategies for dealing with prescription painkiller abuse. According to NIDA, it is difficult to develop and send effective messages to the public. But as long as the messages are well-constructed and scientifically based, it will be hard for people to ignore them. Similar to the issue of pain management, education about prescription painkiller abuse must target all segments of society, including health care providers and the pharmaceutical industry.

 ## Text-Dependent Questions

1. What is "safe use" of prescription painkillers?
2. What non-opioid medications does the CDC recommend for common chronic pain conditions?
3. How can the pharmaceutical industry contribute to future developments for pain management?

Research Project

Explain "substance use disorder" as defined in SAMHSA's 2014 National Survey on Drug Use and Health (http://www.samhsa.gov/data/sites/default/files/NSDUH-FRR1-2014/NSDUH-FRR1-2014.pdf). Look up the number of people, for each of the three age categories, who had a pain reliever use disorder in 2014. Compare the results with the statistics given for heroin use disorder. Write a summary of your findings.

Series Glossary

analgesic—any member of a class of drugs used to achieve analgesia, or relief from pain.

central nervous system—the part of the human nervous system that consists of the brain and spinal cord. These are greatly affected by opiates and opioids.

dependence—a situation that occurs when opiates or opioids are used so much that the user's body adapts to the drug and only functions normally when the drug is present. When the user attempts to stop using the drug, a physiologic reaction known as withdrawal syndrome occurs.

epidemic—a widespread occurrence of a disease or illness in a community at a particular time.

opiates—a drug that is derived directly from the poppy plant, such as opium, heroin, morphine, and codeine.

opioids—synthetic drugs that affect the body in a similar way as opiate drugs. The opioids include Oxycotin, hydrocodone, fentanyl, and methadone.

withdrawal—a syndrome of often painful physical and psychological symptoms that occurs when someone stops using an addictive drug, such as an opiate or opioid. Often, the drug user will begin taking the drug again to avoid withdrawal.

Further Reading

Colvin, Rod. *Overcoming Prescription Drug Addiction: A Guide to Coping and Understanding*. Nebraska: Addicus. 2008.

Klein, Arthur, and Dava Sobel. *Backache: The Complete Guide to Relief*. London: Robinson. 2006.

Meier, Barry. *Pain Killer: A "Wonder" Drug's Trail of Addiction and Death*. New York: Rodale Inc. 2003.

Pinsky, Drew, et al. *When Painkillers Become Dangerous: What Everyone Needs to Know About OxyContin and Other Prescription Drugs*. Minnesota: Hazelden. 2004.

Quinones, Sam. *Dreamland: The True Tale of America's Opiate Epidemic*. New York: Bloomsbury. 2015.

Stolberg, Victor B. *Painkillers: History, Science, and Issues*. California: ABC-CLIO. 2016.

Taylor, Donald R. *Managing Patients with Chronic Pain and Opioid Addiction*. New York: Springer. 2015.

Internet Resources

http://paindatabase.nih.gov/

The Interagency Pain Research Portfolio database enables searches of over 1,200 research projects through a multitiered system. Topics are organized into themes, such as pain mechanisms, overlapping conditions, disparities, risk factors, and training and education.

http://www.painmed.org/

The American Academy of Pain Medicine's website provides current and relevant information on pain medicine, including clinical reference resources and the latest news on pain research.

http://www.cdc.gov/az/p.html

The Centers for Disease Control and Prevention website contains an A-Z index that offers comprehensive information on health topics, including painkiller overdose.

http://www.ccsa.ca/

This website delivers a wide range of publications on substance abuse in Canada. Subjects relate to prescription drugs, alcohol, youths, treatment, impaired driving, prevention, and standards—among others.

http://www.samhsa.gov/

A vast amount of research related to opioids and other substances can be performed on the Substance Abuse and Mental Health Services Administration website. The website also provides resources on national strategies and initiatives, state and local initiatives, and training and education.

https://www.cihi.ca/en

The Canadian Institute for Health Information website offers a National Prescription Drug Utilization Information System (NPDUIS) Database that stores pan-Canadian information on public drug programs.

http://www.ncsl.org/

The National Conference of State Legislatures website houses a myriad of data on U.S. state policies, including prevention of prescription drug overdose and abuse.

Index

Numbers in **bold italic** refer to captions.

About the Author

Grace Ferguson is a writer who lives in Georgia. Her academic writings for students and researchers include *Adolescents* (The SAGE Encyclopedia of Pharmacology and Society), *Temperament* (EBSCO), and *Asian American Leadership: Voter Registration and Voting* (Mission Bell Media).

Picture Credits: Drug Enforcement Administration: 16, 21, 22, 25, 28, 36, 46; © OTTN Publishing: 13, 14, 45; used under license from Shutterstock, Inc.: 1, 2, 6, 8, 32, 38, 48; Helga Esteb / Shutterstock.com: 12 (top); Everett Collection / Shutterstock.com 12 (bottom); A. Katz / Shutterstock.com: 51; Lenscap Photography / Shutterstock.com: 26; United Nations photo: 18.